FLORIDA

Wholesale real estate. Wholesaling houses for beginners

How to find, finance & rehab wholesale properties

By

Fleming Merrill

Table of Contents

Chapter 1 State of Florida Overview

Chapter 2 How To Purchase Investment Property

Chapter 3 Finding Wholesale Investment Property

Chapter 4 REAL ESTATE FINANCING 4,000 Sources!

Chapter 5 Find Florida Wholesale Real Estate Fast!

Chapter 6 Florida Real Estate Investing City Goldmines

Chapter 7 Colossal Cash from Crowd Funding

Chapter 8 Business Insurance

Chapter 9 Rehabbing Real Estate

Chapter 10 HOW TO SELL YOUR PROPERTY FAST!

Chapter 1

State of Florida Overview

State of Florida Overview

Florida is spanish for "land of flowers". One of the things that makes Florida a great place to be a real estate investor is that it has a population of 21,299,325 (2018 est.) the third highest in the United States! The Florida median household income is in the top 50 nationwide with $52,594, which is ranked number 40.

Other nice facts about Florida:

Spoken languages: Predominantly English and Spanish

Motto: In God We Trust

State song: Old Folks at Home

State Nickname: The Sunshine State

State Anthem: Where the Sawgrass Meets the Sky

State Capital: Tallahassee

Biggest city: Jacksonville

Biggest metro: Miami

Area: 65,757.70 sq mi

Ranked: 22 nationwide

State of Florida Overview

Any business person, especially a real estate investor, wants to have a business where the customer base has plenty of money. Another thing that makes Florida's a fantastic place to be an investor is it's $1.0 trillion economy. It is the fourth largest in the United States. If Florida was a country, it would be the 16th largest economy in the world, as well as the fifthty eighth most populous as of 2018. More great invesor numbers...In 2017, Florida's per capita personal income was $47,684, ranking 26th in the nation.

In 2018 Florida ranked 18th in the United States with an unemployment rate at only 3.5 percent.

The Miami economy has the 12th highest gross domestic product in the United States at $345 billion dollars.

Tampa Bay has the 2nd largest economy in the state with a gross domestic product of $145 billion dollars.

Is there money in Florida? Over fifty billionaires call the state of Florida home.

Florida has a high population growth and what seems to be, a never ending amount of new construction!

State of Florida Overview

Walt Disney World, Universal Studios, Busch Gardens and Fun Spot are just a handful of the amusement parks that help to drive the Florida economy. The state's economy also relies on agriculture, transportation, crops of oranges, and the Kennedy Space Center.

Florida is known all over the world as the place to be to play golf, tennis, and enjoy a ton of water sports. Several beaches in Florida have turquoise and emerald-colored coastal waters. Siesta Key beach in Florida made the Travel Channels list as one of the top beaches in the world. It has a 99 percent quartz base sand that remains cool to the touch and feels like baby power when walked on!

The year round warm weather makes Florida a popular destination for retirees.

As an investor, speaking spanish would give you a great business advantage as Florida has a large spanish speaking Latino community. But Florida is diverse with African, European, and indigenous heritage as part of it's landscape.

Chapter 2

How To Purchase Investment Property

Expert Strategies to Purchase Property

Expert Strategies to Purchase Property

AVOIDING & MANAGING & ELIMINATING RISK

Legendary Real Estate investor Dave Del Dotto once said "stick with the government, they will make you rich.". Real Estate is one of the safest investments in the world, when done properly. There is risk just driving to the grocery store. The only thing separating you from a head on collision is a yellow strip of paint. That being said, there are risks in every financial investment decision you make.

Do your research. Know what you want to do, before you begin. Are you looking to flip properties? Hold on and make money on the interest rates? Are you looking for a property to live in? Are you looking to rent out properties? Each decision requires a different type of research. If you are looking to rent out properties then you need to research what the local apartment complexes and homes are renting for in the area. If you are looking to flip a property then you need to find a real estate agent that can give you comps that have sole in the area within the past year.

Visit any property you are going to purchase. You do not want to get stuck with swampland or a unbuildable lot.

Expert Strategies to Purchase Property

AVOIDING & MANAGING & ELIMINATING RISK

You also don't want to get stuck with a property that has high property taxes. Learn the property tax rates of all the counties in the state that you are going to invest in.

Make sure that the property has not been condemned.

Make sure that the property does not have numerous costly violations of city codes.

Ask multiple real estate agents for information on any area you are interested in investing.

Ask about possible environmental issues.

Research possible liens by builders and contractors.

Beware of a owner who may declare bankruptcy on a property. This is a manageable risk but because laws change constantly, consult a real estate attorney for more information on how to handle this risk.

Avoid scams by dealing with government employees as much as possible.

Expert Strategies to Purchase Property

1. Decide how much you can afford to invest and stick with the numbers you come up with. Avoid something called Auction fever. It can be started by a "fast hammer". A fast hammer is when the auctioneer closes the auction early at a amazing price. It is designed to get your attention and get a fever about being the next one in the room to get a "Great Deal". When you go to a auction you should have a list of properties you have research and what your bid is going to be. This will help you to avoid Auction Fever.

2. Research. Single family homes with at least 3 bedrooms are great investments if purchased at the right price. Your research tells you what the right price is. Remember to use real estate agents and their access to the multiple listing service. Also many big companies like Remax and Century 21 have websites up with tons of information on the real estate area you wish to invest in.

www.trulia.com

www.zillow.com

www.biggerpockets.com

https://www.census.gov/quickfacts/table/PST045216/00

http://www.realtor.org

Those are just a few of the great sites to get research information on real estate.

Expert Strategies to Purchase Property

3. Get in contact with local counties for a list of delinquent properties for sale. Also ask when the sales will take place. Ask if you can be put on a mailing list. Use the internet to track down as much information as you can. Don't be afraid to use search engines other than Google. Bing and Yahoo are also great search engines to use.

4. Buy from other investors. Some people get in over their head. As long as you know the numbers and have research the property, it does not matter who you purchase it from as long as it is a good deal. One investor in Michigan recently purchased every single property for sale at a tax auction. He has to sell those properties or he is responsible for paying the taxes. As Carelton Sheets once said "you can't rationalize murder" so how can you rationalize why someone might offer you a great deal? Just do your due diligence on the property before making a deal.

5. Establish a relationship with local officials. Learn the names of the people who work in government offices that will be giving you information. Visit in person and say thank you. Call and say thank you. Send them a card that says thank you. How many people do you think do that for them? They will remember you. I worked for the government for over 20 years. I still remember the woman who repeatedly gave me lemon-aid when it was hot outside.

Expert Strategies to Purchase Property

6. Buy early in the Year. When you buy a tax lien certificate, back taxes have to be paid to the treasurer as well as interest and penalties. Redeem the property and you could be earning interest on this larger amount of money. If the property is not redeemed you can turn in the tax lien certificate and be handed a deed for the property, any extra amount you pay for the certificate comes from you because you could have gotten the same property for less.

7. Try smaller counties you may have much less competition.

8. Invest in your comfort zone. Try to find mentors who have already done what it is you want to do. As your knowledge and experience increases then you can take on bigger projects.

9. Write down your goals. Remember to answer the question of why you are doing this in the first place. A powerful why will keep you motivated when it comes time to do the legwork required to be successful.

10. Take Action. There are plenty of smart people who are poor. Proper Knowledge plus action is the key to success.

Expert Strategies to Purchase Property

In microeconomics total cost (TC) describes the total economic cost of production and is made up of variable costs, which vary according to the quantity of a good produced and include inputs such as labor and raw materials, plus fixed costs.

In English... you factor in as many external costs, not just the cost of the investment property.

In order to be successful when buying investment property, you have to be good at determining the Total Cost of a property.

11. Get Investment Property Market Value

Wholesale Real Estate is real estate that is real estate priced under it's retail value. But how do you know that the retail value of real estate property? The standard formula for finding the value of real estate is to have a real estate agent find comparable (comps) properties that have sold recently. Usually about 4 properties with in a mile of the purchase property, that have sold within the past year. Formulas vary from bank to bank and real estate agent to real estate agent.

Today you can get a rough estimate by doing the research yourself. Remember that a bank will probably use their own formula, but at least you can try to get a ball park figure of a properties value by using these web sites.

Expert Strategies to Purchase Property

Appraisal Web Sites

https://www.zillow.com/how-much-is-my-home-worth/

http://www.eppraisal.com/

12. Selecting a Real Estate Agent

So now that you have found a property, researched it's value, it's time to make an offer. Some times you have to use a government approved agent to make an offer. Like any profession, there are good agents and not so good agents.

When I lived in Virginia, once a year the local paper published a list of all the top real estate agents for almost every real estate agent franchise/business. If your local paper does not do that then here is a formula I use for selecting a real estate agent.

Expert Strategies to Purchase Property

No part timers. Part time effort usually gets you part time results. I want an agent whose livelihood depends on their success.

Size Does Matter

The size that matters. The size or amount of properties sold. Not necessarily the gross amount of property value sold. Suppose you had a real estate agent who sold 1 million dollars worth of real estate and another who sold $500,000 worth of real estate. Which one do you choose? It depends. I want the agent who has sold the most individual properties, and not necessary the one who has the highest gross. An agent can sell only 1 house for a million dollars. The agent who sold $500,000 worth of real estate may have sold 10 $50,000 homes.

Usually a agent who makes a lot of sales has a good marketing formula in place and a good team of agents working with or for her/him. Don't be afraid to ask "who's your best agent? Why?". Often a real estate company will try to toss their worst agent a bone. Don't be that bone. Remember they work for you. Their commission comes from the property you are investing in.

Some courses teach you to negotiate the commission. I believe a proficient agent is worth the commission they desire. It's your job to select a proficient agent.

Expert Strategies to Purchase Property

13. "100-3" Formula

Here is a quick and easy formula for getting a great deal on a real estate investment property, using a real estate agent that you have build up some rapport with.

Have the agent find 100 properties for sale that have been on the market for at least 90 days. Have the agent fax an offer of 25% below market value to all of the properties. Because the properties have been on the market for at least 90 days, you are dealing with motivated sellers. It is likely that 10 out of the 100 will accept your offer. Now filter through the 10 and select the best 3 properties. Use these filters to help you select the best 3.

Strategies To Making Offers

1. What are the property taxes?

2. Are there any Homeowner Association dues?

3. What will be the appreciation value?

4. What will be your utility expenses.

5. How much will it cost, to be "live-in" ready.

6. Is it the lowest valued house in the neighboorhood?

7. What is the Crime Rate

Expert Strategies to Purchase Property

Property Taxes

I once owned two homes free and clear. The homes were in the same state. Both were similar in size, but one had a $3,000 a year property tax and the other one was $300 a year in property taxes. You can guess which one I moved first. Property taxes are often overlooked, but can be a big factor in the (TC) total cost. Do your research before you make an offer.

HOA (Home Owner Association)

Usually when a house seems like the perfect deal, but has been sitting on the market for a long time, look to see what the HOA dues are. Personally I stay away from any property that has HOA dues, because they can escalate and you have no control over them.

Appreciation

Look at the history of real estate appreciation. It can vary greatly form city to city, and neighborhood to neighborhood. If you are going for a quick flip then this is not that important.

Utility Expenses

The importance of the expense depends on what you are going to do with the property.

Expert Strategies to Purchase Property

Rehab Expenses

If you are not an expert, have a professional inspect the house so you can factor in, a accurate estimate of rehab expenses. Be aware of any possible code violations as well.

Cost relative to the Neighborhood

Usually it's easiest to sell the cheapest house in the most expensive neighborhood. However if you just plan on renting the house then this is not as big a factor.

Crime Rate

The crime rate can have a big impact on resale value. Use web sites like https://www.crimereports.com/ to help understand it's impact on your property.

Expert Strategies to Purchase Property

14. "Take what the defense gives you"

Take what the defense gives you is a sports metaphor for viewing the landscape of a situation and adapting to what you see.

Take a similar approach to making offers in real estate. If you tell a "For Sale By Owner" everything that is wrong with the house he or she spend a lifetime building... you may insult the owner and lose the deal.

However, you send a list of needed repairs to a HUD representative, he may reduce the price of the property, no questions asked.

Adjust your offer making strategy to the person or organization you are dealing with. The farther removed a person is from the property, the less emotional they are about making deals.

Know your profit numbers and stick to them. Especially if you are bidding on a property. Be aware of Auction fever. It will bring out the competitive nature in you and can lead to you over bidding on a property. Know your numbers and be disciplined. The reason you pick out 3 properties in the 100-3 formula is so that you have 2 other properties to go to, if your first choice does not work out.

Chapter 3

Finding Wholesale Investment Property

How to Find Wholesale Residential & Commercial Real Estate

How To Find Wholesale Real Estate

There are several basic methods to find real estate at wholesale prices. There are foreclosures and pre-foreclosures, so get excited! There are hundreds of great deals just waiting for you to find them! The first method is Searching Public Records.

Searching Public Records

Go to your county's recorders office and look for notice of default or notice of sale. The advantage of this method is that many newly posted properties have not been seen by your competition. The disadvantage is that it usually takes more time to find property than the other methods.

Here is a tip. When ever a county clerk helps you, get that person's name and thank them face to face. Then go home and call the office and thank them again. Wait about a week. Then purchase a thank you card and mail it. Your kindness is going to stand out to that clerk. In turn that clerk is not likely to forget you. You in turn will likely have an ally in that office. The old saying "It's not what you know, but who you know." This method helps the clerk and yourself get to know each other quicker than usual. At the very least, you should feel good for being a nice person!

How To Find Wholesale Real Estate

Another advantage to searching public records is Probate Properties. You will need to be educated in your local area's probate laws to purchase those properties.

Probate is required for all estates that are not protected by a trust. The average duration of probate is 7 to 8 months.

If the house is owned outright, the estate is responsible for remitting property taxes and insurance premiums throughout the probate process.

Estate administrators can elect to sell the property if it is causing financial harm to the estate. If the estate does not have sufficient funds to cover outstanding debts, the probate judge can order the property sold.

How a probate house is sold depends on the type of probate that is used. "Court Confirmation" is the most common type of probate used. A judge must approve all of the aspects of the management of the estate. Independent Administration of Estate's Act (IAEA) governs the 2nd type of probate administration. It allows estate executors to engage in estate administrative affairs without the court management.

How To Find Wholesale Real Estate

To purchase probate property you have to know which probate system is being applied. Properties can be bought directly from the estate executor when Independent Administration of Estate's process is in effect. You can place your bid through the court system when court approval is required.

An investor interested in finding probate real estate must research public records. When people pass away their last will and testament is recorded in the probate court. The last will and testament will contain valuable information such as the estate assets, who is the beneficiary, and contact info for whoever is administrating for the estate.

Property records should show if there are any liens on the property and if so, who holds the lien. They should also show the properties appraised value, the year it was constructed, the square footage and the lot size. The records may also help you to determine if there have been any tax liens placed on the property.

Do your due diligence when purchasing any type of real estate. Bring in professional help in the form of building inspectors, lawyers and any other professionals that can help protect you when needed.

How To Find Wholesale Real Estate

Using the Internet

I will provide you with a Small Real Estate Rolodex of web sites later in this chapter. Many are completely free and have tons of information. One success algorithm for buying a property is that you should never, never, purchase one property without looking at, at least 100 other properties. Being able to search online makes using this formula very easy.

Using Local Papers and Journals

Local papers and journals. By law many foreclosures have to be posted in the local paper. This can mean a goldmine of opportunity for you. With newspaper circulation in decline, many people are simply not looking in the newspaper anymore. Advantage you.

Next I am going to cover several categories of real estate sources.

* **Nationwide banks & Foreclosure Properties**

* **Government Foreclosure Properties**

* **Commercial Real Estate**

* **FSBO - For Sale By Owner**

How To Find Wholesale Real Estate

Nationwide Banks & Foreclosure Properties

Bank of America

http://foreclosures.bankofamerica.com/

I have purchased property using this web site. It is my favorite because they have a large nationwide inventory and their web site is easy to navigate and sort properties.

Wells Fargo

https://reo.wellsfargo.com/

Place yourself on their mailing list, and get property updates on a monthly basis.

Ocwen Financial Corporation

http://www.ocwen.com/reo

Founded in 1988 they are one of the largest mortgage companies in America.

How To Find Wholesale Real Estate

Hubzu

http://www.hubzu.com/

Hubzu is a nationwide real estate auction web site. Very easy to use. This is a great web site for comparing property prices nationwide.

How To Find Wholesale Real Estate

Government Foreclosure Properties

One advantage purchasing from the government is that there is no emotional attachment to the property. Don't be afraid to make a offer that is lower than the listed price. I once argued with a real estate agent who refused to place a offer lower than the stated price. Eventually I got him to place the offer. (Remember that they work for you, however some government properties can't be purchased unless you go through a HUD or government approved agent.) It was countered twice, before I decided to purchase another property. But they countered with two offers lower than the listed price.

If you are reading a ebook version of this book then you should be able to access these web sites by clicking the links below. But if you are reading a paperback version of this book then be careful when looking for government properties. There are many web sites pretending to be government web sites and some will attempt to charge you fees for information about government properties.

How To Find Wholesale Real Estate Government Foreclosure Properties

Fannie Mae
The Federal National Mortgage Association

https://www.fanniemae.com/singlefamily/reo-vendors

Department of Housing and Urban Development

https://www.hudhomestore.com/Home/Index.aspx

The Federal Deposit Insurance Corporation

https://www.fdic.gov/buying/owned/

The United States Department of Agriculture

https://properties.sc.egov.usda.gov/resales/index.jsp

United States Marshals

https://www.usmarshals.gov/assets/sales.htm#real_estate

How To Find Wholesale Real Estate Commercial Real Estate Properties

City Feet

is a nationwide database of Commercial Real Estate Property

http://www.cityfeet.com/#

The Commercial Real Estate Listing Service

is a nationwide database of Commercial Real Estate Property

https://www.cimls.com/

Land . Net

is a nationwide database of land, commercial real estate for sale and for lease.

http://www.land.net/

Loop . Net

is a nationwide database of Commercial Real Estate Property

http://www.loopnet.com/

How To Find Wholesale Real Estate

FSBO – For Sale By Owner

By Owner

http://www.byowner.com/

For sale by owner in Canada

http://www.fsbo-bc.com/

For sale by owner Central

http://www.fsbocentral.com/

For sale by Owner: world's largest FSBO web site

http://www.forsalebyowner.com/

Ranch by owner

http://www.ranchbyowner.com/

Chapter 4

REAL ESTATE FINANCING 4,000 Sources!

8 Realistic Ways to Finance Real Estate

FINANCING REAL ESTATE

Welcome to Expert financing. I am going to show you several realistic ways to finance real estate. You are going to learn how to finance real estate with.

* VA LOANS

* PARTNERS

* INVESTMENT CLUBS

* CREDIT CARDS

* CORPORATE CREDIT

* EQUITY

* SELLER FINANCE

* HARD MONEY LENDERS

* AND FINALLY I SHOW YOU THE MONEY$!!

USING A VA LOAN

According to the web sites www.benefits.va.gov and www.military.com the current VA Loan amount is a whopping $417,000! What a lot of veterans don't know is that you can use that money to purchase not only your home, but investment properties. That is how I started my investing career. Purchasing multiple homes using my VA Loan.

FINANCING REAL ESTATE

Even if you are not a veteran, you can still partner up with one, who still has some money left on his or her VA LOAN.

If you are a Veteran, you will need to obtain a copy of your DD 214 and VA Form 26-1880 Request for a Certificate of Eligibility.

PARTNERS

This is another way I purchased a home. At the time I worked for the United States Postal Service. I had already purchased plenty of homes, so many of the workers were aware I had successfully invested in real estate. At break time I went around and ask people to partner up with me. I had multiple people offer to go in as a partner. I choose one and that house we rehabbed and flipped just two months after purchasing it. To this day it was the biggest gross profit on one deal, I have had. True I had to split it with my partner, but I would rather have half of something than all of nothing.

Having the combined resources of two people can be a great benefit, but it is not without it's challenges. If you are going to use a partner, no matter how close you are...GET EVERY THING IN WRITING.

FINANCING REAL ESTATE

Having a partner can dramatically increase the chance of a Bank lending money as well as having someone to split the work on rehabbing, should you decide to save money and make repairs yourself. But all this must be spelled out BEFORE you enter into a Agreement/Contract and purchase a home.

It helps if the person is like minded and understands the risks and benefits of investing, and truly understands the return on investment of a particular deal.

REAL ESTATE INVESTMENT CLUBS

Real estate investment clubs are groups that meet locally and allow investors and other professionals to network and learn. They can provide extremely useful information for both the novice and expert real estate investor. A top real estate club can provide a great forum to network, learn about reputable contractors, brokers, realtors, lawyers, accountants and other professionals. On the other hand, there are many real estate clubs designed to sell you. They bring in "gurus" who sell either on stage or at the back of the room, and as a result, the clubs typically profit to the tune of %50 of the sale price of the product, bootcamp, or training that is pitched.

FINANCING REAL ESTATE

I have purchased a ton of real estate books and real estate courses. Carlton Sheets, Dave Del Dotto, The Mylands, Seminar courses and much much more. I am not against any club bringing in a speaker who has a course. However I think there should be transparency to the members of the club.

There is certainly value in the networking that may come at one of these groups. But attend working to attain your goals and not necessarily the club's goal to sell you something. Some times both are the same thing. As a rule I usually leave debit cards at home the first time I attend an event. If there is a seller there with a "This day only offer" then I won't feel pressured to purchase. Plus most sellers can be convinced to sell at the discount offer price at a later time when you have had a chance to come down off the "sense of urgency emotional pitch" .

CREDIT CARDS

When using a credit card in real estate you must really do your homework on the deal. Dan Kennedy a world famous marketer once said "always stack the numbers in your favor". That's how you use a credit card. Look at the return on investment as compared to the long term cost of using a credit card and it's interest. Also I would recommend buying low cost homes that you can purchase and own free and clear.

FINANCING REAL ESTATE

No Mortgage Payment!!! My last 2 homes I have purchased have been cash deals. One home cost $1,500 and the other about $7,000. The first was a government property from HUD and the 2nd From a Bank. These institutions are unemotional about real estate and simply view a property as a non performing asset. The 2nd home was 4 bedrooms, 1 1/2 bath and a basement located in a farming community and came with a 2 car garage/shed and .6 acre(that is the size of a NFL football field) of land.

In this book I show you how to find plenty of houses with amazing below wholesale prices and a formula for almost always finding a great deal.

CORPORATE CREDIT

Many people set up corporations to buy and sell real estate as an additional protection against liabilities. Other's create a corporation to mask personal involvement in property transfers and public records. Regardless of the use of a corporation, you can buy real estate with corporate credit as an alternative to using your own cash or IRA. By capitalizing on the credit rating of your corporation, you can buy real estate and build your corporate holdings portfolio.

FINANCING REAL ESTATE

Just remember that you can set up your corporation in a state that favors you the most for your real estate deals. Do your research. Most people like Delaware and Nevada, but you will have to decide if your home state or any other state is best for you and your business.

CURRENT EQUITY

Using the equity in your home for real estate investing is another way you can finance properties. You might use the money for a down payment or it may only be enough to cover the cost of some rehab repairs.

If you stick to the low cost home formula, you may have enough to purchase the entire house. A house is an investment that should appreciate in value as well as give a great ROI (Return On Investment). When you decide to flip the property or rent it out for positive cashflow.

If you have equity and it's not doing anything, then you may decide to make it a "performing asset" and use it as part of your real estate finance program.

FINANCING REAL ESTATE

SELLER FINANCING

Seller finance is where the seller of a free and clear property becomes your bank along with being the seller.

Advantages:

You get to purchase the property on terms that may be more beneficial for you. Seller gets monthly payments and the benefit of treating the sale as an installment sale thus allowing them to defer any capital gains taxes that may be due.

Disadvantages:

You may be locked into a mortgage with a pre-payment penalty or may not be able to resell the property immediately. This strategy is typically not meant for flipping but can definitely be used for that purpose if structured correctly.

Seller Finance is a known way to finance a property. That is why I have presented it in this book. But it is my least favorite because you now have a lingering relationship with your property. Your ability to make decisions regarding the property is limited and for that reason, I would not go this route. However, like all types of financing, you have to ask yourself, "is the deal worth it."

FINANCING REAL ESTATE

I also prefer to work alone, but when a great deal came along, I sought out a partner to make it happen. Risk is usually relative to potential profit.

HARD MONEY LENDERS

A hard money lender is usually a individual or company that lends money for an investment secured by the investment property.

Advantages:

Less red tape to get the money. You are dealing with people who understand the real estate investment business.

Disadvantage:

This is not a long term loan. The lender wants a return on investment, usually within a few months, a a year, or a few years. The interest rate on the loan is much higher than usual conventional banks.

Using hard money has a higher risk because the return on investment is due quicker. Therefore it is a good idea not to use a Hard Money Lender, until you have a great deal of experience and confidence in being able to produce a return on investment.

SHOWING YOU THE MONEY

A list of web sites for financing.

www.businessfinance.com (4,000 sources of money!)

www.advanceamericaproperty.com

http://www.cashadvanceloan.com/

www.brookviewfinancial.com

www.commercialfundingcorp.com

www.dhlc.com
(hard money for the Texas area)

www.equity-funding.com

www.bankofamerica.com

www.carolinahardmoney.com
(for real estate investors in North and South Carolina)

www.fpfloans.com

FINANCING REAL ESTATE

As you can see there are plenty of strategies for financing a property. Do your research on your investment property and get the true market value. Purchase well below wholesale. This will help to minimize risk and elevate your potential profit margins. Buying below wholesale also creates a buffer for unexpected expenses.

So don't let the lack of money be a roadblock in your real estate investing dreams.

Chapter 5

Find Florida Wholesale Real Estate Fast!

Find Florida Wholesale Real Estate Fast!

The internet has made it possible to grow your real estate investing business quickly and easily. Now you can view a hundred houses online without ever leaving your home.

In this chapter I am going to give you a ton of web sites and the addresses to government wholesale sources, to help you to cover this state's real estate goldmines. I have selected some of the biggest counties with the largest supply of wholesale real estate.

In general you should look at 100 homes for every 1 property that you purchase. Comparing factors like the home value, rent potential, repair cost, local taxes, possible home owner fees, utilities etc...

While there is no substitute for inspecting a home in person, having access to thousands of homes on the internet can help you to narrow down the field to spectacular deals! So take advantage of this knowledge to help secure your real estate investing success!

Find Florida Wholesale Real Estate Fast!

Locate Statewide Florida Properties

MLS.com

This web site has Florida Real Estate Foreclosures with links to different cities on the landing page.

http://www.mls.com/search/florida.mvc

REALTOR.com

This web site has Links to Florida real estate properties by county and city.

http://www.realtor.com/foreclosures/Florida

Top Florida Counties

The previous web sites give you access to a broad selection of property in all 67 counties in Florida.

Next I narrow it down to a handful of the top counties based on the population size, rising property values, rental profit potential and the abundance of wholesale property available.

Find Florida Wholesale Real Estate Fast!

Miami-Dade County

Miami-Dade County has a population of 2,662,874 and is 1,946 square miles. The best Goldmine investment oppurtunities in this county are Miami and Hialeah.

Delinquent Taxes and Tax Certificate Sales

Miami-Dade County Tax Collector

140 West Flagler St., 1st Floor, Suite 1407, Miami, FL 33130

Phone: (305) 375-5452

Tax Certificate Information:

https://urlzs.com/StaQr

Auction Web site:

https://bidmiamidade.com/

Tax Deed Sales:

https://urlzs.com/nsPcP

Find Florida Wholesale Real Estate Fast!

Broward County

Broward County has a population of 1,780,172 and is 1,209 square miles. The best Goldmine real estate investment oppurtunities in this county are Fort Lauderdale.

Delinquent Taxes and Tax Certificate Sales

Broward County Revenue Collector

Broward County Governmental Center Annex

115 South Andrews Avenue, Fort Lauderdale, FL 33301

Phone: (954)831-4000

Foreclosure Sales

https://www.broward.realforeclose.com/index.cfm

Tax Deed

https://broward.deedauction.net/

Tax Lien

https://www.bidbroward.com/

Find Florida Wholesale Real Estate Fast!

Hillsborough County

Hillsborough County has a population of 1,267,775 and is 1,051 square miles. The best Goldmine real estate investment oppurtunities in this county are in Tampa.

Tax Certificate Sales

Hillsborough County Tax Collector
601 E. Kennedy Blvd., 14th Floor, Tampa, FL 33602
Phone: (813) 635-5200 Fax: (813) 612-6707

Foreclosure:

https://www.hillsborough.realforeclose.com/index.cfm

Tax Deed Sale Information:

https://urlzs.com/rrKtU

Find Florida Wholesale Real Estate Fast!

Orange County

Orange County has a population of 1,169,107 and is 908 square miles. The best Goldmine real estate investment oppurtunities in this county are in Orlando.

Orange County Tax Collector
200 South Orange Ave., Suite 1500, Orlando, FL 32802
Phone: (407) 836-2700

Government Foreclosures:

https://www.myorangeclerk.realforeclose.com/index.cfm

Tax Sales:

http://www.octaxcol.com/tax-certificate-deed-sales/

https://www.occompt.com/official-records/tax-deed-sales/

Find Florida Wholesale Real Estate Fast!

Pinellas County

Pinellas County has a population of 917,398 and is 280 square miles. The best Goldmine real estate investment oppurtunities in this county are in Petersburg.

Pinellas County Tax Collector
29399 US Highway 19 N, Suite 100, Clearwater, FL 33761
Phone: (727) 464-7777

Government Foreclosures:

https://www.pinellas.realforeclose.com/

Tax Sales:

https://taxcollect.com/tax-certificate-deed-sales/

Find Florida Wholesale Real Estate Fast!

Duval County

Duval County has a population of 870,709 and is 918 square miles. The best Goldmine real estate investment oppurtunities in this county are in Jacksonville.

Duval County Tax Collector
231 E. Forsyth St., Jacksonville, FL 32202
Phone: (904) 630-1916

Government Foreclosures:

https://www.duval.realforeclose.com/

Tax Sales:

https://duvalfl.realtaxlien.com/

Find Florida Wholesale Real Estate Fast!

Lee County

Lee County has a population of 631,330 and is 804 square miles. The best Goldmine real estate investment oppurtunities in this county are in **Cape Coral**.

Lee County Tax Collector
2480 Thompson St., Fort Myers, FL 33902
Phone: (239) 533-6000

Government Foreclosures:

https://www.lee.realforeclose.com/index.cfm

Chapter 6

Florida Real Estate Investing City Goldmines

Florida Real Estate Investing
City Goldmines

1. Jacksonville

The city of Jacksonville has a population of 867,313 to support your real estate investing business.

The **median home value** in Jacksonville is $177,500. Jacksonville is a real estate goldmine city because recently the home values have gone up 8 percent and is expected to rise at least another 4 percent.

Houses currently listed in Jacksonville have a median list price of about $220,000. Homes that actually sold have a median price of about $160,000.

The **median rent price** in Jacksonville is about $1300. This ranks #6 between Florida Goldmine Cities.

Foreclosure Warning sign

Delinquent mortgages in Jacksonville is 1.9 percent. The *Foreclosure potiential rank is #1 between Florida goldmine cities.*

Florida Real Estate Investing
City Goldmines

2. Miami

The city of Miami has a population of 443,007 to support your real estate investing business.

The **median home value** in Miami is $337.200. Miami is a real estate goldmine city because recently the home values have gone up 2.8 percent and is expected to rise at least another 0.4 percent.

Houses currently listed in Miami have a median list price of about $475,000. Homes that actually sold have a median price of about $312,000.

The **median rent price** in Miami is about $2,430. This ranks #1 between Florida Goldmine Cities.

Foreclosure Warning sign

Delinquent mortgages in Miami is 1.2 percent. The *Foreclosure potiential rank is #6 between Florida goldmine cities.*

Florida Real Estate Investing
City Goldmines

3. Tampa

The city of Tampa has a population of 368,087 to support your real estate investing business.

The median home value in Tampa is $221,100. Tampa is a real estate goldmine city because recently the home values have gone up 5.5 percent and is expected to rise at least another 1.6 percent.

Houses currently listed in Tampa have a median price of about $335,000. Homes that actually sold have a median list price of about $214,000.

The median rent price in Tampa is about $1,600. This ranks #4 between Florida Goldmine Cities.

Foreclosure Warning sign

Delinquent mortgages in Tampa is 1.3 percent. The *Foreclosure potiential rank is #4 between Florida goldmine cities.*

Florida Real Estate Investing
City Goldmines

4. Orlando

The city of Orlando has a population of 269,414 to support your real estate investing business.

The median home value in Orlando is $241,200. Orlando is a real estate goldmine city because recently the home values have gone up 6.7 percent and is expected to rise at least another 2.8 percent.

Houses currently listed in Orlando have a median price of about $290,000. Homes that actually sold have a median list price of about $248,000.

The median rent price in Orlando is about $1,600. This ranks #4 between Florida Goldmine Cities.

Foreclosure Warning sign

Delinquent mortgages in Orlando is 1.2 percent. The *Foreclosure potiential rank is #6 between Florida goldmine cities.*

Florida Real Estate Investing

City Goldmines

5. Hialeah

The city of Hialeah has a population of 237,523 to support your real estate investing business.

The median home value in Hialeah is $286,300. Hialeah is a real estate goldmine city because recently the home values have gone up 8.4 percent and is expected to rise at least another 3.0 percent.

Houses currently listed in Hialeah have a median price of about $319,950. Homes that actually sold have a median list price of about $253,000.

The median rent price in Hialeah is about $2,000. This ranks #2 between Florida Goldmine Cities.

Foreclosure Warning sign

Delinquent mortgages in Hialeah is 1.3 percent. The *Foreclosure potiential rank is #4 between Florida goldmine cities.*

Florida Real Estate Investing
City Goldmines

6. Tallahassee

The city of Tallahassee has a population of 188,463 to support your real estate investing business.

The median home value in Tallahassee is $183,400. Tallahassee is a real estate goldmine city because recently the home values have gone up 6.9 percent and is expected to rise at least another 2.8 percent.

Houses currently listed in Tallahassee have a median price of about $225,000. Homes that actually sold have a median list price of about $189,100.

The median rent price in Tallahassee is about $1,100. This ranks #7 between Florida Goldmine Cities.

Foreclosure Warning sign

Delinquent mortgages in Tallahassee is 1.4 percent. The *Foreclosure potiential rank is #3 between Florida goldmine cities.*

Florida Real Estate Investing
City Goldmines

7. Port St. Lucie

The city of Port St. Lucie has a population of 178,778 to support your real estate investing business.

The median home value in Port St. Lucie is $222,500. Port St. Lucie is a real estate goldmine city because recently the home values have gone up 7.0 percent and is expected to rise at least another 3.0 percent.

Houses currently listed in Port St. Lucie have a median price of about $247,000. Homes that actually sold have a median list price of about $211,000.

The median rent price in Port St. Lucie is about $1,625. This ranks #3 between Florida Goldmine Cities.

Foreclosure Warning sign

Delinquent mortgages in Port St. Lucie is 1.6 percent. The *Foreclosure potiential rank is #2 between Florida goldmine cities.*

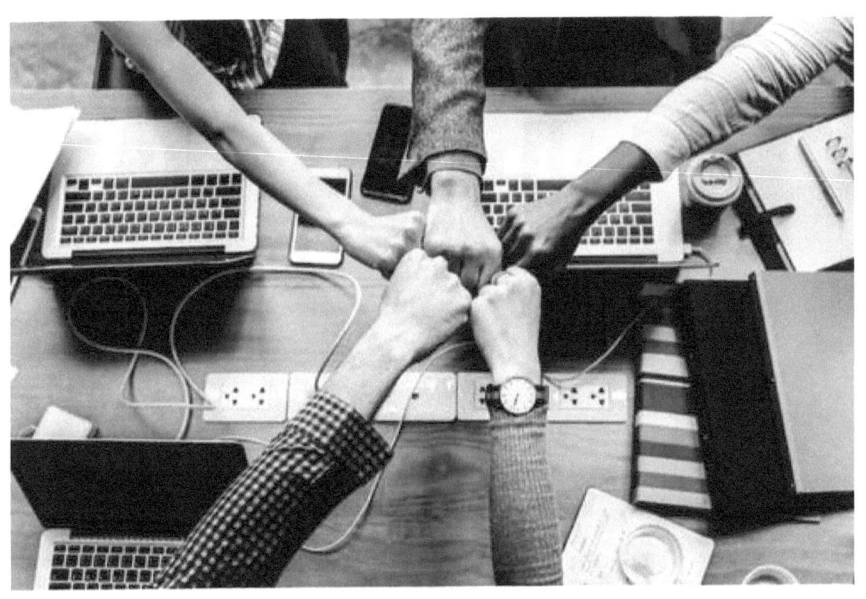

Chapter 7

Colossal Cash

from

Crowd Funding

Crowd Funding Crowd Sourcing

In 2015 over $34 billion dollars was raised by crowdfunding. Crowdfunding and Crowdsourcing roots began in 2005 and they help to finance or fund projects by raising money from a large number of people, usually by using the internet.

This type of fundraising or venture capital usually has 3 components. The individual or organization with a project that needs funding, groups of people who donate to the project, and a organization sets up a structure or rules to put the two together.

These websites do charge fees. The standard fee for success is about %5. If your goal is not met there is also a fee.

Below is a list of the top Crowdfunding websites according to myself and Entrepreneur Magazine Contributor Sally Outlaw.

Crowd Funding Crowd Sourcing

https://www.indiegogo.com/

Started as a platform for getting movies made, now helps to raise funds for any cause.

http://rockethub.com/

Started as a platform for the arts, now it helps to raise funds for business, science, social projects and education.

http://peerbackers.com/

Peerbackers focuses on raising funds for business, entrepreneurs and innovators.

https://www.kickstarter.com/

The most popular and well know n of all the crowdfunding websites. Kickstarter focuses on film, music, technology, gaming, design and the creative arts. Kickstarter only accepts projects from the United States, Canada and the United Kingdom.

Crowd Funding Crowd Sourcing

Group Growvc

http://group.growvc.com/

This website is for business and technology innovation.

https://microventures.com/

Get access to angel investors. This website is for business startups.

https://angel.co/

Another website for business startups.

https://circleup.com/

Circle up is for innovative consumer companies.

https://www.patreon.com/

If you start a YouTube Channel (highly recommended) you will hear about this website frequently. This website is for creative content people.

Crowd Funding Crowd Sourcing

https://www.crowdrise.com/

"Raise money for any cause that inspires you." The Landing page slogan speaks for itself. #1 fundraising website for personal causes.

https://www.gofundme.com/

This fundraising website allows for business, charity, education, emergencies, sports, medical, memorials, animals, faith, family, newlyweds etc...

https://www.youcaring.com/

The leader in free fundraising. Over $400 million raised.

https://fundrazr.com/

FundRazr is an award-winning online fundraising platform that has helped thousands of people and organizations raise money
for causes they care about.

CHAPTER 8
Business Insurance

BUSINESS INSURANCE

Consult an attorney for any and all of your business matters.

In the early 1990's an elderly woman purchased a hot cup of coffee from a McDonald's drive-thru window in Albuquerque. She spilled the coffee, and suffered 3rd degree burns. She sued Mcdonald's and won. She won 2.7 million dollars in a punitive damages victory. The verdict was appealed and settlement is estimated at somewhere in the neighborhood of $500,000 dollars. All because she spilled the coffee into her lap, while trying to add sugar and cream.

Two men in Ohio, were carpet layers. They were severely burned when a three and a half gallon container of carpet adhesive ignited, when the hot water heater it was sitting next to, was turned on. They felt the warning lable on the back of the can was insufficient. So they filed a lawsuit against the adhesive manufacturers and were awarded nine million dollars.

A woman in Oklahoma, purchased a brand new Winnebago. While driving it home, she set the cruise control to 70 miles per hour. She then left the drivers seat to make some coffee or a sandwich in the back of the motor home.

BUSINESS INSURANCE

The vehicle crashed and the woman sued Winnebago for not advising her, that cruise control does not drive and steer the vehicle. She won 1.7 million dollars and the company had to rewrite their instruction manual.

Unfortunately all three outrageous lawsuits are real. If you are going to run a business, any business, you should consider protecting yourself with Professional Liability Insurance, also known as Errors and Omissions (E & 0) insurance.

This type of insurance can help to protect you from having to pay the full cost of defending yourself against a negligence lawsuit claim.

Error and Omissions can protect you against claims that are not usually covered in regular liability insurance. Those policies usually cover bodily harm, or damage to property. Error and Omissions can protect you agaist negligence, and other mental anguish like inaccurate advice, or misrepresentation. Criminal prosecution is not covered.

Errors and Ommision insurance is recommended for notaries public, real estate brokers or investors and professionals like: software engineers, lawyers, home inspectors web site delvelopers and landscape architects to name a few professions.

BUSINESS INSURANCE

The Most Common Errors and Omission Claims:

%25 Breach of Fiduciary Duty

%15 Breach of Contract

%14 Negligence

%13 Failure to Supervise

%11 Unsuitability

%10 Other

BUSINESS INSURANCE

Things you should know about or require before purchasing a Errors and Omission policy is...

* What is the limit of liability

* What is the Deductible

* Does it include FDD First Dollar Defense - which obligates the insurance company to fight a case without a deductible first.

* Do I have Tail-end coverage or Extended Reporting Coverage (insurance that lasts into retirement)

* Extended coverage for Employees

* Cyber Liability Coverage

* Department of Labor Fiduciary Coverage

* Insolvency Coverage

If you get Errors and Omission insurance, renew it the day it expires. You must be careful to avoid gaps in your coverage, or it could result in not getting your policy renewed.

BUSINESS INSURANCE

A few E & O Insurance Providers:

Insureon

Insureon states that their median Errors and Omissions Insurance policy cost about $750 a year or about $65 a month. The price of course will vary according to your business, the policy you choose and other risk factors.

https://www.insureon.com/home

EOforless

EOforless.com helps insurance, investment, and real estate professionals buy E & O insurance at an affordable cost in five minutes or less.

https://www.eoforless.com/

BUSINESS INSURANCE

CalSurance Associates

As a leading insurance broker, CalSurance Associates, a division of Brown & Brown Program Insurance Services, Inc. has over fifty years of experience delivering comprehensive insurance products, exceptional service, and proven results to over 150,000 insured. They provide professionals nationwide and across multiple industries, including some of the largest financial firms and insurance companies in the United States.

http://www.calsurance.com/csweb/index.aspx

Better Safe Than Sorry

Insurance is one of the hidden costs of doing business. These are just a few companies and a brief overview on the topic of business insurance. Make sure to talk to an attorney or quailified insurance agent before making any decision on insurance. Protect you and your business. Many states do not require E & O insurances. But when you see the cost of some of the settlements, it's better to be safe than sorry.

Chapter 9

Rehabbing Real Estate

Rehabbing Real Estate

There are three basic components to rehabbing a property. Have a property inspection, a cost analysis and hire a contractor.

A. Home Inspection

You can hire a licensed professional to inspect the propery or you can do it yourself. I advise hiring a licensed professional with a great deal of experience.

To hire a professional you can google "home inspection, your city, your state" or go to homeadvisor.com.

http://www.homeadvisor.com/

https://goo.gl/vL4gWK

If you choose to do it yourself here is a basic home inspection checklist.

Rehabbing Real Estate

Exterior

* **Roof:** Determine if the roof needs repairs or needs to be replaced.

* **Lawn:** Determine what kind of landscaping is needed or if the yard needs to be reseeded.

* **Sprinkler:** Is there a sprinkler system? If so does it work?

* **Lights:** Do the lights work? Are there motion sensors? Are there cost efficient bulbs?

* **Outlets:** Do the outlets work?

* **Fence:** Does it need repair or painting?

* **Trees:** Do any trees need to be removed or trimmed?

* **Garage Door:** Does it open and close easily?

Rehabbing Real Estate

Overall Interior

* **Walls:** Do they need paint or repair?

* **Floors:** Do tiles or carpet need to be replaced? Do wood floors need to be repaired?

* **Stairs:** Are the stairs sturdy? Do they make noise. Is the handrail sturdy and safe?

***Outlets:** Purchase a voltage tester and see if all the outlets work.

* **Doors:** Do they open and close easily? Are they level?

***Windows:** Do you feel any breezes when you stand by them? Are they cost efficient?

***Lights:** Turn on every light switch to make sure they work. (Note: If the home is unoccupied and the power is turned off, this won't be possible.)

Rehabbing Real Estate

Kitchen

* **Countertops:** Check for chips and cracks.

* **Cabinets:** Do they open and close easily? Do they need to be refinished or replaced?

* **Oven:** Does the oven work? Is it outdated?

* **Refrigerator:** Check to see if it freezes. Does it pass the eyeball test or is it an eyesore.

* **Faucet:** Run the water in the sink. Any leaks? How is the water pressure?

* **Range Hood:** See if the range hood fan and light work. It most likely will need to be cleaned.

Rehabbing Real Estate

Bathrooms

* **Plumbing/Drainage:** Fill up the sink and tub and see how the water drains out.

* **Faucets:** Check for leaks.

* **Toilet:** Is there enough pressure when it is flushed?

* **Bath Tub:** Is it too small? Any scratches?

* **Ventilation:** Does the fan work? Is there a window? Does it open and close easily?

Bedrooms

* **Closets:** Is there enough space? Are hanger rods needed?

Rehabbing Real Estate

Living/Dining/Family Room

* Ceiling Fans: Do ceiling fans need to be added or replaced?

Basement

* Mold: If there is an odor, check for mold and mildew.

* Furnace: Does the furnace work? Is it outdated? Up to code?

* Water Heater: Check for water around the base of the water heater. Any stickers on this to indicate installation date?

A documentary about Walt Disney revealed that Walt purchased a home for his parents and a faulty gas furnace was the cause of his mother's death. So inspecting a house can be a life or death matter.

You can use this checklist to determine your offer price and begin a overall cost analysis. However it is highly recommended that you use a professional.

Rehabbing Real Estate

B. Cost Analysis

When investing in real estate, you should always stack the numbers in your favor. If you can purchase a property at %50 of it's wholesale value, then you leave enough margin for error to absorb expenses and still sell the property for a profit.

The real estate web site biggerpockets.com has a investment calculator that can do the cost analysis work for you.

https://www.biggerpockets.com/real-estate-investment-calculator

https://goo.gl/HFoK9x

Rehabbing Real Estate

However you can do a quick cost analysis yourself. Here are the basic numbers you will need.

* after repair value

* desired profit

* estimated repair cost

* purchase closing cost

* sale closing cost

* agent commission

* monthly holding costs

* number of days it will take to rehab and sell

Take the "after repair value" and substract all of the expenses.

Rehabbing Real Estate

C. Hire a Contractor

It is a good idea that you hire a contractor. However if you decide to do the repair work yourself there is a supply discount program from Home Depot.

WHAT IS IT?

You have to get their Pro Xtra Account. If you're spending at least $1,500, chances are you can save money. In select markets, you may only need to spend only $1,000. Check with your local store to confirm required purchase amount.

HOW DOES IT WORK?

Assemble your project list. Build your cart in the store. If your total adds up to at least $1,500 (or $1,000 in select markets, check with your local store), you probably qualify for a volume discount.

Quotes can be processed by the Pro Desk any time and most requests are priced immediately. Membership in Pro Xtra Loyalty Program is required to receive discounts.

Full details are at the web site listed below...

http://www.homedepot.com/c/Pro_VolumePricing

Rehabbing Real Estate

A. How to Find a good Contractor

Go to your local building material warehouses like Lowes, Home Depot, Menards and Sherwin Williams.

Ask them who are their high volume contractors. If contracters are frequently purchasing supplies then they are frequently working. This is one of the more reliable ways to find a quality contractor.

Ask other contractors. Often times you will come across a good contractor who is busy on another project. Ask him/her for recommendations.

Ask a high volume real estate agent. Top real estate agents usually know one or two good contractors.

Use the internet.

Google "contractors, your city, your state".

Use homeadvisor.com

Try angieslist.com

Rehabbing Real Estate

B. Contractor Checklist

Hiring the right contractor can make or break a deal. Remember they work for you, so don't be shy about asking questions and getting proof, BEFORE you sign a contract. Here is a question checklist.

1. Do you have a license bond and insurance?

Do You Carry General Liability Insurance?

- It is Best to find a remodel contractor that carries general liability insurance.

2. Do you have referrals?

Do not hesitate to call referrals. - Nice to get several customer references from the last 6 months to one year.

3. Can I get a detailed and comprehensive scope of work with the bid?

4. Ask about experience and verify if you can.

Rehabbing Real Estate

5. Who's doing the work and who's going to be the daily contact on the project?

- Make sure the contractor or his foreman is on the job whenever work is being performed.

6. Will You Pull All the Required Building Permits?

- Pulling the required building permits, you know things will be done to "code."

7. Do You Guarantee Your Work?

Your contractor should guarantee his work for at least one year from date of completion. They should also include any warranties from the material used if applicable.

8. How do you handle clean up?

Clean up can be expensive. You need to know if the best options are being used.

Rehabbing Real Estate

9. How Is Payment Handled?

- Per job?

- Upon completion?

- Weekly?

- Some money upfront?

- Do you have capital to buy materials in case we need you to?

These are basic questions that you should be asking to interview contractors before you begin any job. Hiring the right contractor can go a long way in giving you peace of mind, when you are a Real Estate investor.

Chapter 10

HOW TO SELL YOUR PROPERTY FAST!

12 Steps to Selling Any Property Fast!

HOW TO SELL YOUR PROPERTY FAST!

12 Steps to Selling Any Property Fast!

1. Clean and Paint the house

Make sure the house is clean and uncluttered. This makes it easier for a buyer to envision themselves living there. Make the bathrooms and kitchen a priority.

2. Scent the house

You might use a light incent or get some vanilla extract and place it on a old school lightbulb to give it a fresh baked cookie smell.

3. Write a property description

Writing a great property description is key to getting buyers interested in your home. One short cut to learning how to write a good property description is to view property listings of sold properties.

4. Take Good pictures

If you don't have a good camera, buy one. A picture is worth a 1,000 words.

HOW TO SELL YOUR PROPERTY FAST!

12 Steps to Selling Any Property Fast!

5. Send a email to your buyers list

If you do not have a buyer's list, here is a link to a complete set of training videos on how to build a valuable customer list.

https://urlzs.com/6Q2uQ

6. Post ads on craigslist

Keep reposting your ads on a daily basis so that you stay at the top of the search results.

7. Post ads to Backpage

http://www.backpage.com/

This is a Worldwide Classified Ad Web Site.

HOW TO SELL YOUR PROPERTY FAST!

12 Steps to Selling Any Property Fast!

8. Place a Ad on http://realeflow.com/

This is the number one source for real estate investing leads.

9. visit the zillow rental manager https://www.zillow.com/rental-manager/

This is a free rental web site.

10. Create a video virtual tour

Create a video virtual tour and upload the video to YouTube. This is a powerful tool. YouTube is 2nd only to Google as the largest Search Engine in the world. However just posting a video won't get it seen. It has to be Search Engine Optimized(SEO). Below is a link to training videos that will show you step by step how to create great videos and get massive traffic viewing them!

https://urlzs.com/6Q2uQ

HOW TO SELL YOUR PROPERTY FAST!

12 Steps to Selling Any Property Fast!

11. Post an ad on facebook target a city

You can place an ad on Facebook and target the city that your property is in.

12. Place a Standard For Sale sign in the yard

If possible have flyers available as well.

13. Place addition white signs in the yard

Give more information and get more attention by placing more personal signs in the yard.

14. List the property in the MLS

If you are not a real estate agent get one to do it for you.

HOW TO SELL YOUR PROPERTY FAST!

12 Steps to Selling Any Property Fast!

15. Place directional signs

Help people find your house. Make sure you are not violating any county codes when placing signs.

16. Continue marketing until closing

Don't slack off. If necessary you might want to hire VA's Virtual Assistants to keep all ads running.

17. Eliminating Negative Cash Flow

https://www.airbnb.com/

Airbnb is a web site that markets your house or rooms in your house for rent. It's easier to sell your house when it is clean, empty and buyers can envision themselves living in it.

However, if you are suffering from negative cash flow you might want to look into just renting out 1 room in the house.

HOW TO SELL YOUR PROPERTY FAST!
12 Steps to Selling Any Property Fast!

In Summary

1. Clean and Paint the house

2. Scent the house

3. Write a property description

4. Take Good pictures

5. Send a email to your buyers list

6. Post ads on craigslist

7. Post ads to http://www.backpage.com/

8. Place a Ad on http://realeflow.com/

9. https://www.zillow.com/rental-manager/

10. Create a video virtual tour

11. Post an ad on facebook target a city

12. Place a Standard For Sale sign in the yard

13. Place addition white signs in the yard

14. List property in the MLS

15. Place directional signs

16. Continue marketing until closing

17. Rent on Airbnb to eliminate negative cashflow

Take these steps to sell your property and you stack the odds in your favor for a quick property sale!

www.ingramcontent.com/pod-product-compliance
Lightning Source LLC
Chambersburg PA
CBHW021848170526
45157CB00007B/2987